Managing Your Money
Planning Your Budget

by Barbara Brooks Simons

Table of Contents

PURCHASED FOR YOUR SCHOOL WITH
FUNDING FROM CONSUMER CREDIT
COUNSELING SERVICE OF **MD & DE** INC.
www.cccs-inc.org

For more information:
www.econed.org

A **resource** helps people do something or get something. Money is a resource. People earn money and spend money in different ways.

Look at these photographs.

How are people spending money?

The _____ is _____.

How are people earning money?

The _____ is _____.

Why do people earn money?

---

resource – what people can use to do something or get something

at the bank

at the doctor's office

at the mall

at the office

CHAPTER 1

Earning, Spending, Saving

Every day people buy and sell **goods** and **services**. A good is an item that people make. Food and clothing are goods. Phones, cars, and books are goods, too.

A service is a type of work that people do for others. Giving someone a haircut is a service. A doctor's work is also a service.

goods – items that people make

services – types of work that people do for others

People use money to buy goods and services. So people find ways to earn money. The money they earn is their **income**.

How do young people earn income? Some young people have part-time jobs. Some baby-sit or help their neighbors with chores. Sometimes young people receive money from their families. Money from all of these sources is income.

income – money earned by working or received from another source, such as a gift

This young woman works part-time. In other words, she works a few hours each week at this store.

KEY IDEAS People use money to buy goods and services. The money that people earn by working or from other sources is called income.

Needs and Wants

When people have an income, they can make decisions about how to spend their money. They can decide how to spend their money by thinking about their **needs** and **wants**.

Needs are goods and services that people must have to live. Goods such as food and clothing are needs. Services such as healthcare are also needs.

Wants are goods and services that people would like to have, but do not need to live. Goods such as **expensive** jeans are wants, not needs. Services such as music lessons are wants, not needs.

needs – goods and services that people must have to live

wants – goods and services that people would like to have, but don't need

expensive – costing a lot of money

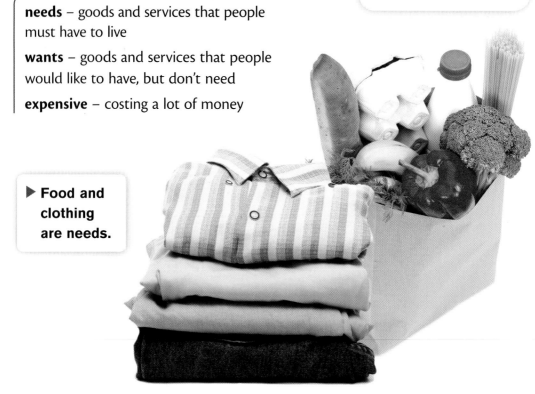

▶ **Food and clothing are needs.**

Buying Goods and Services

Most people keep some of their income as **cash**. They can pay for goods and services immediately with cash.

Sometimes people have a **checking account** at a **bank**. They **deposit** money in the checking account. Then they write **checks** to pay for goods and services. Each check tells the bank how much money to pay to a company or a person.

cash – money; bills and coins

checking account – an account that allows a person to write checks

bank – a place where money is kept for saving and lending

deposit – put money into a bank account

checks – pieces of paper that tell a bank to pay a certain amount of money

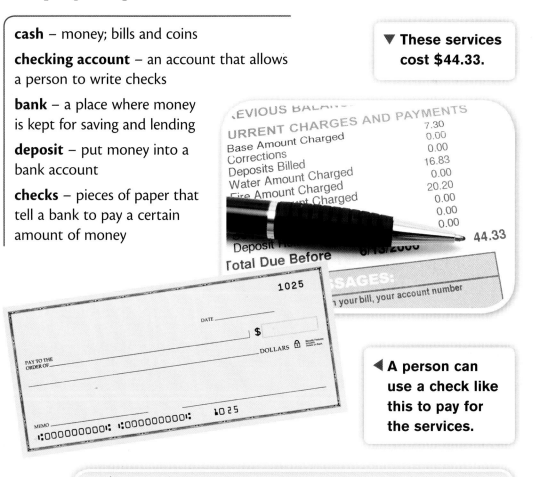

▼ **These services cost $44.33.**

EVIOUS BALAN
URRENT CHARGES AND PAYMENTS
Base Amount Charged 7.30
Corrections 0.00
Deposits Billed 0.00
Water Amount Charged 16.83
Fire Amount Charged 0.00
nt Charged 20.20
.... 0.00
.... 0.00
.... 44.33
Deposit
Total Due Before

1025

SAGES:
your bill, your account number

DATE

$

DOLLARS

PAY TO THE ORDER OF

MEMO

1025

◀ **A person can use a check like this to pay for the services.**

> **KEY IDEAS** People spend money on needs and wants. People pay for goods and services in different ways.

Saving Money

Banks offer **savings accounts** as well as checking accounts. A savings account is for money that is not needed right away. People use savings accounts to save money.

Banks pay **interest** on the money in a savings account. The interest payment is a percentage of the amount in the savings account. The money in a savings account increases with each interest payment.

savings account – a bank account that pays interest on the money in it

interest – payment for the use of money; usually a percentage of the total amount

By The Way...

About 45% of Americans do some of their banking online.

KEY IDEA People use savings accounts to save money and earn interest.

ANALYZE CAUSE AND EFFECT

A cause makes an event happen. An effect is the result of the event. Complete the chart below with an event and an effect. Think of other examples.

Cause ⟶	Event ⟶	Effect
I needed money for guitar lessons.	I saved some money.	I can take guitar lessons this summer.
I got $30 for my birthday.		

MAKE CONNECTIONS

Do you and your classmates think the same way about spending and saving? How are your ideas about money alike? How are they different?

USE THE LANGUAGE OF SOCIAL STUDIES

What types of services are needs?

The services provided by doctors and dentists are needs.

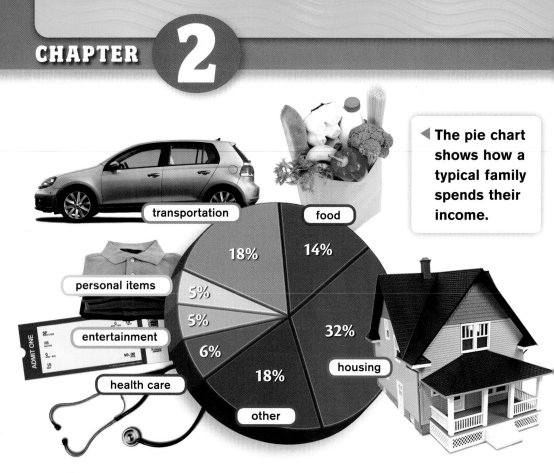

CHAPTER 2

The pie chart shows how a typical family spends their income.

transportation 18%

food 14%

personal items 5%

5%

entertainment

6%

18%

other

32%

housing

health care

Planning a Budget

People earn, spend, and save money. People need a plan for their money, or a **budget**. A budget shows a person's income and **expenses**.

Expenses are the money that is spent on goods and services. On a budget, expenses are divided into **categories**, such as housing and food.

budget – a plan for using money wisely

expenses – the money spent on goods and services

categories – groups of items that are alike in some way

Miranda's Budget

Most young people depend on their family for basic needs, such as food, clothing, and a place to live. But young people can plan budgets, too.

A budget is an important step in learning to use money wisely. Miranda starts her budget by writing down what her income is every month.

▼ **Miranda is starting to plan a budget.**

Income

$25.00 per month
from baby-sitting

$15.00 per week
from parents

Miranda's next step is to put her expenses into categories. She chooses these categories: school, personal items, fun, and gifts. Then she lists items for each category. She marks each item as a need or a want. Miranda also adds a category for savings.

Expenses

Category	Examples	Need	Want
school	supplies	X	
	club dues		X
	bus pass	X	
	lunch	X	
personal items	jewelry		X
	cosmetics		X
fun	snacks		X
	music		X
	video games		X
gifts	gifts to others		X
	contributions		X
savings		X	

▲ Do you agree with the items that Miranda marked as needs?

Next, Miranda creates a monthly budget. Miranda begins by listing her sources of income. She earns $25 each month from baby-sitting. Her parents give her $15 each week. So her income is $85 per month.

Then, Miranda lists her expenses. She begins with her needs. She names each item and tells how much it costs.

Miranda's budget shows that her needs cost $60 each month. Since her income is $85, she has $25 each month for her wants. She can buy music or snacks. She can use this money for gifts.

Monthly Budget

Income		Expenses	
baby-sitting	$25	lunches	$30
money from		supplies	$5
parents	$60	bus pass	$15
		savings	$10
Total	$85	Needs	$60
		Wants	$25
		Total	$85

Miranda earns more income in some months. She gets gifts of money for her birthday. Some months she earns more than $25.00 from baby-sitting. Miranda deposits the extra income into her savings account.

Miranda has more expenses in some months. She buys gifts for her friends' birthdays. Sometimes she must pay for special events at school. She uses money from her savings account to pay for these extra things.

Every month, Miranda uses her budget to keep track of her income and expenses.

KEY IDEA A budget helps a person make wise decisions about spending and saving money.

INTERPRET DATA

Monthly Family Budgets			
Family and Number of People	Housing (rent)	Food	Transportation
Family A, two people	$450	$225	$65
Family B, four people	$950	$300	$105

The chart shows what two families spend on housing, food, and transportation each month. Use the information in the chart to answer the questions.

1. How much does Family A spend on housing, food, and transportation in three months?

2. Family B has an income of $2,000 per month. How much money do they have each month after they pay for housing, food, and transportation?

MAKE CONNECTIONS

Find out what it costs to ride the bus where you live. How much would it cost each month to ride the bus every day?

 STRATEGY FOCUS

Determine Importance

Look at this chapter again. What are the most important ideas? How do you know?

CHAPTER 3

Making Decisions About Money

For most people, money is a limited resource. In other words, most people have a limited amount of money. They cannot buy everything that they want and need. So people have to make choices.

For example, Sam received $50 for his birthday. He wants a video game. He also wants a new backpack. But Sam doesn't have enough money to pay for both. So Sam has to make a choice.

Explore Language

Opposites

limited = restricted; having only a certain amount

limitless = without limits; having an endless amount

Sam knows that he will have to give up either the video game or the backpack. In other words, his decision will have an **opportunity cost**. If he chooses the video game, the opportunity cost will be the backpack. If he chooses the backpack, the opportunity cost will be the video game. Sam makes a chart about his choices.

opportunity cost – the cost of the good or service you must give up when you decide to buy a different good or service

Choices	Cost	Decision	Opportunity Cost
I can buy a new backpack.	$35		
I can buy a new video game.	$50	✓	I will not buy a new backpack.

KEY IDEAS Because money is a limited resource, people must make decisions about spending and saving. Every decision has an opportunity cost.

How to Make Good Decisions

Questions like these can help a person make wise decisions about spending and saving.

- What do I want to buy?
- Is it a need or a want?
- How important is it to me?
- What is the opportunity cost of buying the good or service?
- Do I have the money in my budget to buy this item right away?
- If not, how long will it take me to save the money?

KEY IDEA Asking questions can help a person spend and save money wisely.

MAKE DECISIONS

Look at the two situations on the chart. How would you decide what to do? What would you decide? With a partner, discuss the questions you would ask yourself about each choice. Make a decision about each situation.

Situation	Choice 1	Choice 2	My Decision
1	I can go to a movie with a friend.	I can baby-sit and earn money.	
2	I can buy three songs by my favorite group.	I can buy a ticket to their concert.	

MAKE CONNECTIONS

Look at the decisions you made in the activity above. With a partner, discuss the opportunity costs of each decision you made.

EXPAND VOCABULARY

The word **save** can be used in many contexts. Discuss the different meanings of **save** in these sentences.

I will **save** $10 each month.
Josh **saved** the ball during the game.
Can you **save** a place for me?

Working Toward Your Future

What types of jobs do you do now?

Your work can help you develop new skills.

These skills can help you with a future career.

Your Job Now	Skills
counselor at day camp	• organizing schedules and planning activities • keeping people safe • working well with managers and children
cutting grass and cleaning yards	• organizing appointments • finding new clients • completing jobs on time
selling ads for school paper	• handling money • creating and writing ads • meeting deadlines

Read the chart. Think about work that you do.

Discuss these questions with a partner.

• How will these skills help me in the future?

• How can I learn other skills?

• What job do I want in the future?

Words that Compare

You can use **more**, **most**, **less**, and **least** to compare things.

Words such as **more** and **less** help compare two things.

Words such as **most** and **least** help compare three or more things.

EXAMPLES

I spend **more** money on clothes than on snacks.

I spend the **most** money on school lunches.

June saves **less** money than Carlos, and Bryce saves the **least** of all.

Talk About It

With a partner, talk about Miranda's budget on page 13.

Compare the cost of each item listed in the budget.

Use **more**, **most**, **less**, and **least**.

Write a Comparison

Write about how you spend money.

- Compare how much you spend on needs with how much you spend on wants.

- Explain your goal. What would you like to spend less on? What would you like to spend more on?

Words You Can Use	
Comparison Words	
more	less
most	least

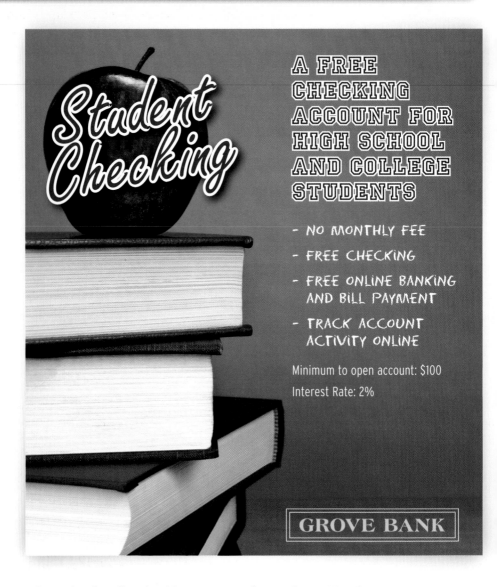

Some banks offer checking accounts for students. Use the information above to answer these questions.

- Who can open one of these accounts?
- What interest rate is offered?
- Do you think this is a good checking account for students? Explain why or why not.

budget (budgets) a plan for using money wisely
A family **budget** includes food, rent, and healthcare.

expense (expenses) money spent on a good or a service
She wrote her **expenses** as needs and wants in her budget.

good (goods) an item that people make
Clothing, shoes, and books are **goods**.

income money earned by working or from another source such as a gift
She earned a good **income** by working at the bank.

interest payment for the use of money; usually a percentage of the total amount
The **interest** on the savings account was 3 percent.

need (needs) a good or a service that a person must have to live
Having a place to live is a **need**.

opportunity cost (opportunity costs) the cost of the good or service you must give up when you decide to buy a different good or service
The **opportunity cost** of buying the computer game is that I won't buy concert tickets.

service (services) a type of work that people do for others
The work a dentist does is a **service**.

want (wants) a good or a service that a person would like to have, but doesn't need
Buying music is a **want**, not a need.

Index

MILLMARK EDUCATION CORPORATION
Ericka Markman, President and CEO; Karen Peratt, VP, Editorial Director; Lisa Bingen, VP, Marketing; Dave Willette, VP, Sales; Rachel L. Moir, VP, Operations and Production; Shelby Alinsky, Associate Editor; Ana Nuncio, Language Editor; Hanneman Productions, Photo Research; Arleen Nakama, Technology Projects

PROGRAM AUTHORS
Mary Hawley, Program Author, Instructional Design
Peggy Altoff, Program Author, Social Studies

STUDENT BOOK DEVELOPMENT Gare Thompson Associates, Inc.

BOOK DESIGN Steve Curtis Design

TECHNOLOGY Six Red Marbles

CONTENT REVIEWER
Margit McGuire, PhD, Program Director and Professor of Teacher Education, Seattle University, Seattle, WA

PROGRAM ADVISORS
Scott K. Baker, PhD, Pacific Institutes for Research, Eugene, OR
Carla C. Johnson, EdD, University of Toledo, Toledo, OH
Margit McGuire, PhD, Seattle University, Seattle, WA
Donna Ogle, EdD, National-Louis University, Chicago, IL
Betty Ansin Smallwood, PhD, Center for Applied Linguistics, Washington, DC
Gail Thompson, PhD, Claremont Graduate University, Claremont, CA
Emma Violand-Sánchez, EdD, Arlington Public Schools, Arlington, VA (retired)

PHOTO CREDITS Cover and 2a ©Bill Aron/Photo Edit; IFC and 15a ©David Safanda/ iStockphoto.com; 1a, 4a, 5a, 8a, 11a, 14a, 16a, 17c, 18a, 23a ©David Young-Wolff/Photo Edit; 2–3a ©LHB Photo/Alamy; 3a ©Ken Lax/Photo Researchers, Inc.; 3b ©Wodicka Erwin/age fotostock; 4b ©Robert Brenner/Photo Edit; 6a and 10a ©Edyta Pawlowska/Shutterstock; 6b ©Grin Maria/ Shutterstock; 7b ©Jill Battaglia/Shutterstock; 7c ©Anthony Berenyi/Shutterstock; 8b ©Clayton Sharrard/Photo Edit; 9a and 9b Photos by Ken Karp; 10b ©Maksim Toome/Shutterstock; 10c Steve Curtis Design; 10d ©Brian Chase/Shutterstock; 10e and 10f©Pertusinas/Shutterstock; 10g ©Milos Luzanin/Shutterstock; 11b ©Lars Lindblad/Shutterstock; 12a ©Elena Itsenko/Shutterstock; 12b, 13b, 17b©Lars Lindblad/Shutterstock; 12c ©thecreativeeyes/Shutterstock; 13a ©Konstantin Yolshin/Shutterstock; 16b ©Tereshchenko Dmitry/Shutterstock; 20a ©Mary Steinbacher/Photo Edit; 21a ©Mike Flippo/Shutterstock; 22a ©Anton Prado PHOTO/Shutterstock; 24a ©Atanas Bezov/Shutterstock

Published by Millmark Education Corporation
PO Box 30239
Bethesda, MD 20824

ISBN-13: 978-1-4334-0655-3

Printed in the USA

10 9 8 7 6 5 4 3 2 1